House of Cards

Drama conceived by

STEPHEN GUNDERSHEIM

Written by

AF278501

Seth Aganski
Tom Austin
Tara Bowman
Sarah Corbin
Emily Dignan
Lee Gabriel
Greg Hall
Amanda Hannoosh
Jaci Keimach
Chris Keyser
Dan LaBroad
Brian Lee
Jennifer MacLean
Andrew Markos
Emily Pierce

Phelan Wolfendon
Adam Yeremian
Amy Bartlett
Anthony Beatrice
Jess Bryant
John Clevesy
Brian Fitzgibbons
Rachel Keimach
Peter Leonard-Solis
Kristin Minichiello
Tiffany Oswiak
Kerrin Rhuda
Cathy Thomas
Stephen Gundersheim

Dramatic Publishing Company
Woodstock, Illinois ● Australia ● New Zealand ● South Africa

IMPORTANT BILLING AND CREDIT REQUIREMENTS

All producers of the play *must* give credit to the author of the play in all programs distributed in connection with performances of the play and in all instances in which the title of the play appears for purposes of advertising, publicizing or otherwise exploiting the play and/or a production. The name of the author *must* also appear on a separate line, on which no other name appears, immediately following the title, and *must* appear in size of type not less than fifty percent (50%) the size of the title type. Biographical information on the author, if included in the playbook, may be used in all programs. *In all programs this notice must appear:*

House of Cards was originally produced at Pentucket Regional High School in West Newbury, Mass., on May 2, 2002. Prompted by an Augusto Boal exercise during Pentucket's advanced acting class, the director conceived this idea for a play using the journal reactions of the class. These initial journal entries were formed into monologues with the class that were edited, rewritten and shaped to become the skeleton of the play that was created by the director and the cast during the rehearsal process. Improvised dialogue became scripted, and the version here is from the final performance.

Cast

The Joker	Emily Dignan
Ace of Spades (AS)	Cathy Thomas
Two of Spades (2S)	Brian Fitzgibbons
Five of Spades (5S)	Jess Bryant
Ten of Spades (10S)	Greg Hall
King of Spades (KS)	Seth Aganski
Four of Diamonds (4D)	John Clevesy
Six of Diamonds (6D)	Peter Leonard-Solis
Jack of Diamonds (JD)	Kerrin Rhuda
King of Diamonds (KD)	Rachel Keimach
Three of Clubs (3C)	Tom Austin
Six of Clubs (6C)	Amy Bartlett
Eight of Clubs (8C)	Anthony Beatrice
Queen of Clubs (QC)	Kristin Minichiello
Ace of Hearts (AH)	Andrew Markos
Seven of Hearts (7H)	Jennifer MacLean
Nine of Hearts (9H)	Tiffany Owsiak
Queen of Hearts (QH)	Amanda Hannoosh

Production Staff

Director .... Stephen Gundersheim
Stage Manager ....Jill Domings
Stage Manager .... Ryan Murray
Light Board .... Mike Barreiros
Spotlight Operator..Will Hall
Spotlight Assistant .... Danielle Dombrowski
Lighting Designer ....Ryan Murry
Sound Engineer... Ryan Murray
Costumer Designer.. Connie Rhuda
Curtain...Jill Domings
Ushers .... Danielle Dombrowski, Leah Sheehan
Poster Designer ....Jill Domings
Public relations...................................Jennifer Leonard-Solis
Refreshments..................................... Theatre Parents Group

To the theatre community of Pentucket,
who made my time there a blessing.

And to Karina and Jackie, who shine from above.

All profits from any royalties will go to scholarships at
Pentucket Regional High School in their memory.

ACKNOWLEDGMENTS

An incredible thanks to Pentucket Regional High School's 2002 advanced acting class for their initial work, commitment and writing, for listening to my and one another's pieces and for helping to shape the monologues.

A special thank you to the cast for their ability to improvise and then set the dialogue for our scenes so that we could take the initial readings from class and create this actual play— you all helped realize my idea into a live production and are co-authors.

Special thanks to Johanna Smith and Barbara Maier for presenting the workshop that prompted me to use the card exercise with my own students, to Jen Leonard-Solis for her time transcribing the scenes for me and to Emily Dignan for all of her work with me on the Joker's monologues; it was a true collaboration.

Another special thanks to Connie Rhuda for the production's costumes, and a special thank you to all the teachers and directors (too many to mention here) who have influenced my work as both a teacher and a director.

Thanks to my colleagues at Pentucket Regional High School, especially my friend Marcia Nadeau-Tanner and my department head and biggest advocate, Ellen Hart. Finally, thanks to my parents who supported me in theatre from my early days and to my wife, Susan, and my children, Hannah, Rebecca and Doron, who make it all worthwhile.

SETTING

House of Cards was originally done on an empty stage with simple lighting effects. Contemporary music was used for the beginning of the play and during the curtain call. A magical bell sound was used each time the Joker froze the action. As a convention, characters remained in the frozen tableaux and would step out to deliver their monologue and then step back in. The cafeteria scene was done by rolling actual tables on-stage from the cafeteria—this is easily borrowed from your own school lunch room.

COSTUMES

Costumes consisted of simple jeans and white T-shirts with each member of the cast wearing a T-shirt with the number and symbol of their card and value (e.g., the number nine with two hearts on a T-shirt can be used for the Nine of Hearts character).

PRODUCTION NOTE

Pop culture references may be altered and updated to current social trends.

House of Cards

CHARACTERS

(7m., 8w., 3 either gender)

JOKER: either gender.

ACE OF SPADES (AS): woman.

TWO OF SPADES (2S): man.

FIVE OF SPADES (5S): either gender.

TEN OF SPADES (10S): either gender.

KING OF SPADES (KS): man.

FOUR OF DIAMONDS (4D): man.

SIX OF DIAMONDS (6D): man.

JACK OF DIAMONDS (JD): woman.

KING OF DIAMONDS (KD): woman.

THREE OF CLUBS (3C): man.

SIX OF CLUBS (6C): woman.

EIGHT OF CLUBS (8C): man.

QUEEN OF CLUBS (QC): woman.

ACE OF HEARTS (AH): man.

SEVEN OF HEARTS (7H): woman.

NINE OF HEARTS (9H): woman.

QUEEN OF HEARTS (QH): woman.

AUTHOR'S NOTES

House of Cards is a piece that came about quite by accident. I led an exercise with my advanced acting class in the fall of 2001 based on a workshop I attended. The session was based on Augusto Boal's work dealing with social issues of power, and we did an exercise with a deck of cards exploring how people treat one another when each card is given a value, thereby creating a social class structure. I asked the students to write a journal entry at the end of the session, and when I read them, I thought that they would make interesting monologues. For two weeks we conferenced in small and large groups to edit these pieces, which were then performed.

I decided to make them into a short play—some of which was created during the rehearsal process with those who are in the cast. The result is a patchwork of individual perspectives on how people are valued in a world or society (in this case, students in a high school). Regardless of whether you or others label you an ace (lowest value) or a king (highest value), we all are equal and, to some extent, misunderstood. *House of Cards* has been an incredible learning experience for me as a director, teacher and playwright (yes, I wrote some of the pieces in the play). I loved collaborating with the students using improvisation to create realistic dialogue within the scenes. I always try to push students to work outside of their comfort zone while still feeling safe. We accomplished this together, and I have thoroughly enjoyed writing, editing, creating and working with these young people. I hope that in these difficult and turbulent times, *House of Cards* will remind us of the value of every human life.

House of Cards

SCENE 1: MORNING ARRIVAL

(Stage is empty. Contemporary music begins playing as ACE OF SPADES enters L and pantomimes opening a locker and taking out a notebook. She then sits down and begins scribbling in the notebook.

SIX OF DIAMONDS enters L and SIX OF CLUBS enters R and meet at imaginary lockers.)

6D. Oh, hey, how's it going?

6C. Not bad, how are you?

6D. Well … all right. So, did you do the math homework?

6C. Do I ever do the math homework? No. *(Pause.)* Can I borrow yours?

6D. Well, what period do you have it?

6C. I don't know, 5th, maybe.

6D. I'll check. It says you have it 3rd and I have it 5th.

6C. I can get it back to you around 4th.

6D. Well, OK.

6C. Thanks. I'm failing that class.

(The other playing cards enter at various points during this conversation—some alone, some in groups. They pantomime typical early morning school activities: going to lockers, unloading backpacks, checking locker mirrors, greeting and talking with friends. Those in groups are segregated by rank—Kings, Queens and Jacks together; Aces, Twos and Threes together, etc.

EIGHT OF CLUBS and NINE OF HEARTS are opening their lockers.)

8C. So, I was waiting at the bus stop this morning when Queen and Jack passed by in Queen's new Camaro; and they laughed at me!

9H. Don't you hate that? I'm so sick of having to wait for the bus. You know the other day when it was raining? Well, I was waiting and there was this huge mud puddle and somebody drove by and splashed water all over me.

8C. Don't you hate when that happens?

9H. Yeah, I had to come to school soaking wet and wait for my mom to bring me some dry clothes.

8C. That stinks!

(TEN OF SPADES approaches QUEEN OF HEARTS at her locker.)

10S. Hey, Queen, did you do that English homework last night?

QH. I don't have to.

10S. Yeah, she'll pass you anyway; she loves you.

QH. Yeah.

(ACE OF HEARTS approaches AS, who is still sitting on the floor scribbling in a notebook.)

AH. You definitely did not do that math homework right.

AS. I didn't?

AH. No. You see, if you square the square root, it cancels out. Then you bring the number on the other side of the equation.

AS. Really?

AH. Yeah.

AS. Thanks.

(THREE OF CLUBS is sitting on the ground near where 8C and 9H are talking at their lockers.)

3C *(calling up to the pair)*. Hi. Hi, Eight. Hi.

(8C pauses a moment, looks disgusted, and then turns back to his conversation.

QUEEN OF CLUBS and QH are at their lockers.)

QC. Does my make-up look all right?

QH. Yeah, it looks fine.

QC. I like your hair.

QH. Thanks.

(6D and JACK OF DIAMONDS pass each other in the hallway.)

6D. Um, hi, Jack. I like your hair.

JD. Thanks. *(To her friends behind 6D's back.)* Are you kidding me?

(QH pushes FIVE OF SPADES out of the way.)

QH. Excuse me!!

(JOKER claps hands and the action freezes.)

JOKER. At this point in time shall our story begin
   About the house of cards and the people within.
   Each occupant bearing upon his breast
   A numerical figure, a value at best,
   To decide where each lies in the grand scheme of things,
   In a place where no mortal of equality sings.
   But of scales, and of levels that separate friends
   Into cheap definitions that each number lends,
   And where intelligence, loyalty or lack of conceit
   Are by one's card value made completely obsolete.
   So, listen closely, my friend, to each Jack, King and Eight,
   And learn your lesson well from the stories they relate.
   So that if one day you find yourself in a judgmental place,
   You can recall just how badly it feels to be an Ace.

*(JOKER claps hands and action resumes. Cards mill around
the stage in small groups or individually as if heading to
class. Wind chime sounds and the action freezes. Through-
out the play, as each monologue is delivered, everyone re-
mains frozen except for the person talking.)*

9H. Today, I was hanging with my usual group, my friends, or so
I thought. I was being quiet, as always trying to blend in, laugh
at the right jokes; my pathetic routine. Then Queen started
telling about her party and everyone joined in with who they
were going with, what they were wearing and other stupid
details like that. I started to say, "I think I'll wear my new red
tank top," when I was told that I was "so not invited" by King,
who was being worshipped by Ten and asked me to leave.
No explanation, just that I was supposed to leave, and like a
coward, I did. I wish I stayed and stood up to King, but I know
I never could. I've had the blow off conversation in my mind
so many times, but I just can't get the strength to stand up to
her. But what bothers me the most is that even though I never
really "fit in" with them, without them, I'm nothing. Nothing
but alone in a school of cliques, best friends and ex-friends. I
guess I'm afraid that things will stay this way forever.

3C. Same old, same old. I come back from the summer vaca-
tion for my senior year and not a single person has changed.
None of the "cool" people will even give me the time of day.
It's our senior year for crying out loud. I thought that people
would actually have matured over the summer. I guess there
is really no use in trying to hang out with the cool people;
they are all so stuck on themselves and each other. At least I
know who my real friends are. So what if we watch reruns of
the original *Star Trek* or play chess against ourselves, just to
see who can beat themselves first. At least it's fun.

4D. Right, so anyway…what am I doing? Packing my backpack! Then why … why am I packing a stuffed octopus? I
guess this might be why everyone thinks of me as eccen-

tric. You know what? I like being me with my stuffed octopus. Everybody knows you need a stuffed octopus for math class, right? And of course I have Phillip, my lucky penny. Phillip is a girl, by the way. She and I have been together since preschool, and guess what? I haven't even been hit by a bus yet! Seriously! Not a single one! Oh, sure, I have been hit by a few cars, but … the face cards were driving them. Yeah, darn face cards! They are deeply involved in a vast left-wing conspiracy designed to destroy me and the other psychopaths. I know it. But really, who wants friends like the face cards when you're more at peace without them? You know what? Yesterday, I heard Phillip talking. She said she was actually an agent for the FBI and that, when I least expect it, she would turn me in to the feds. I think she is delusional. But she listens when I talk … Yeah, Phillip is truly a lucky penny—at least for now. Watch, tomorrow Jack will ridicule me using her third grade vocabulary as we pass each other in the hall. Whatever …

SCENE 2: LUNCHTIME

(JOKER claps, school bell sounds, cards set up lunch tables then exit, leaving JOKER alone onstage.)

JOKER. Lunchtime. Time for the King and time for the Ace
　　To settle on a satisfying, comfortable place
　　Where they can almost feel like they belong.
　　But if this is achieved, it won't stay long.
　　For here in the house of cards, my friend,
　　The firm preconceptions refuse to bend
　　To the way, perhaps, that things should be
　　Without the segregational mentality.
　　But they come, and they sit, if they can find a seat,
　　And it happens each day as the patterns repeat.

(JOKER claps and cards begin entering the lunchroom at various points. Some pantomime carrying trays through the cafeteria line, others go immediately to tables and pantomime eating a brown bag lunch or working on homework, etc. Eventually, the cards are divided into groups at two lunch tables. At one table are KING OF DIAMONDS, KING OF SPADES, QC, QH, JD and 10S, with 9H and 8C further down the table. At the other table are 6D, 6C, 5S, FOUR OF DIAMONDS, 3C, TWO OF SPADES and AH. Some are seated, some are sitting on top of the tables and a few are standing next to the tables.)

QC. OK. So, everybody's coming to my party tonight, right?

(Everyone in the group indicates yes by saying it or nodding.)

KD. What time is it at?

QC. 8 o'clock.

JD *(to QH)*. Oh. Can I have a ride?

QH. I don't know what I'm doing for a ride yet.

(SEVEN OF HEARTS approaches the "cool" table carrying a tray.)

7H. Hey, guys!

10S *(getting up from table and going over to 7H)*. Hi, Seven. Hey, come here for a second. I hate to have to tell you this, but you can't sit with us because we don't have acne.

(Everyone at "cool" table laughs. 7H dejectedly looks around for another place to sit.)

5S *(to 7H)*. Dude. I saw what happened.

7H. Yeah.

5S. Harsh.

7H. Yeah. *(Starts to move away looking for another table.)*

5S *(calling out to 7H)*. Hey! You can sit with us.

7H *(taking one more look around for another table)*. Well, all right. Thanks. *(Sits down.)*

5S. Cool!

AH *(to 7H)*. You shouldn't have to. You know what? None of us should have to. I'm sick of this!

3C. Who do they think they are?

2S. Well, what are we supposed to do about it?

AH. I say we go over there and sit with them anyway.

(AH, 3C and 2S go over and sit at the "cool" table.)

KD *(turning from conversation to notice the new arrivals)*. Something smells.

8C *(standing, whispers to 9H)*.What losers!

3C *(stands to face 8C)*. Do you want to say that to me?

(There is an awkward pause, then KD breaks into a forced laugh and others join in to ridicule 3C.)

JD. Oh, my God! I don't believe he just said that!

(3C and 2S return to the other table. 3C loudly slams his hand on the table in frustration.)

AH *(standing and looking directly at QH)*. That wasn't funny.

(10S moves next to QH facing AH.)

10S *(mockingly)*. That wasn't funny.

(All at the "cool" table laugh. QH moves slightly away from the group with AH.)

QH *(uncomfortably)*. Look, why don't you just go away?

AH *(staring at QH for a moment first)*. Fine, Queen. *(Returns to the other table.)*

(Wind chimes sound and the action freezes.)

JOKER. So you see as I'm sure you already had a hunch.
   Lunchtime is about more than just eating lunch.

10S. You should have seen what happened today. Today was awesome … actually it was better than awesome—it rocked! 'Kay, well you know that new card, Seven or whatever? Yeah, well me, Queen, Queen, Jack and King were all just hanging out and stuff, and Seven totally just came over and tried to be all cool … but she just doesn't understand that she's a Seven and will never be able to hang out with us. So when she came over, I saw this as an opportunity to try and heighten my status with King, so I made my move and told Seven that her face looked like a war zone of acne, and Seven totally walked away from us … it was a really good move on my part, cuz the group totally thought I was cool for it, which pretty much guaranteed myself a spot at the table later in the week at lunch. Nine confronted me the other day and wanted to know why I haven't been hanging out with Nines or Eights lately, and I just told Nine that I didn't like them anymore and did not feel appreciated by them … but the truth is, I never felt under-appreciated or disliked by Eights and Nines … or really by anyone below me, I always felt awesome. They're all really cool and really nice cards, but they don't understand … no one understands … there's always been something missing. Whenever I saw any of the face cards walking in the hall, they always looked different. They always looked special—like they were set apart from everyone else. They always looked so glamorous and, well, famous to an extent … famous in our school, I mean. And all that I wanted was a piece of what they had. And I found the way … I have finally found the key to walking with them in the halls, sitting with them at lunch, going to the mall on weekends … Why should I give that up now? … I do miss them, though … Nine and Eight … and even Six a little … but I can't … that phase, that section of my life is done. What would King and the other face cards think?

(Sigh.) Later, I'm going over to Jack's house—we're going to watch TRL together. God, I hate that show, but imagine … me … at a face card's house! I'll pretend to like it, so that the group doesn't kick me out … then I won't have anybody to sit with at lunch … well, except for Ace, but hell—I don't think even Two or Three would sit with Ace!

2S. You know, being called a loser, geek, scrub and so on can make a person feel terrible. I know, because I've been there. Actually, I'm still there. Other popular people act as if I don't exist. Maybe I don't, in their world. I mean, it's as if they might get shot if they look at me when I pass them in the hallways. If only they'd look closer. However, I do have friends of my own and, though they may not be many, they are friends I can rely on. All in all, I don't care about those "cool" or "popular" people because I have good friends, too. But, you see, the difference between my friends and their friends is, my friends are real and forever.

AS *(looking at KD)*. I wonder what it would be like … to be her. I wonder how I would wake up in the morning. Would my hair be perfect and my make-up pre-applied? Would I look in the mirror and say, "Wow! I look hot today"? Would I know that I would be the dream and the envy of every single person around me? Would I know that I would be worshipped and praised by people like me? That I'm wonderful? That I am the most powerful person in the school? All my friends think I am so strong. They think I don't care what people say about me. I guess I would think the same if a friend of mine acted the way I do, always denouncing *(Points at face cards.)* their superiority. "Who cares if they call me gorilla, right? Who cares if they call me the beast? They're not that wonderful anyway."—I wonder if anyone knows how I really feel; if they know that I would do anything to be like that, like her. I would kill.

6C. I am outta here … this school sucks! I don't care what you think I should wear or who I should be friends with or what I like to do with my free time or what party I am NOT invited to this weekend or why I have no boyfriend or why my parents love my sister more than me or any of it … I'm just so tired. So tired of all this … I feel like all I do is try to impress people and try to be what everyone wants me to be and I am so mixed up that I don't even know who that is or was, or whatever. And I have too much homework and I hate my math teacher and I have no dress to wear to the Spring Fling and my friends all have a different lunch so I am stuck between the Nines and Tens and the Threes and Twos without a place to sit. Can't hang with the Nines and Tens—not good enough for them—and I am NOT gonna be caught with the losers. This year is just like last year—same old crap, different day. I don't think I can take much more of this. My life pretty much sucks. Pretty much.

JD. Wow! I can't believe how cute I look today. I'm just so excited to go to Queen's party tonight. It is going to be so much fun. *(Looking at KS.)* I heard King is going, he is so hot. "Well, hello, Kingy, how are you tonight?" "Me?—Oh. I'm fine." Maybe he would notice me more if I weren't so snobby. You know, it's weird. Because sometimes I wish I had the guts to go up to a loser like Three, and just say hi. I bet she would be so happy. Maybe then they wouldn't think I was such a snob. No, maybe it's not such a good idea. Because then the Kings and Queens may think I was a total geek. I bet if I were King, I could do it, because then I would definitely be at the top. Imagine that, me, Jack, being King. Then I'd let King know how things should go. Then I would be setting all the rules. *(Looking at KD.)* UGH! I hate her so much; she's so damn perfect, even her teeth are perfect. It's so sickening. If I were King, I wouldn't have to worry about anything, well, about what people think about me, anyways. King really has it easy. But I still don't understand why she has to be so cruel. I know this sounds kind of stupid, but if ever I was to become King, I would never be that cruel. I would always smile at everyone, not just at the people of my importance. I could help tutor, and maybe even join a club or two. Then everyone would know I was nice, and not think I was such a snob. Yeah, that would be nice. Well, maybe I don't have a chance at becoming King, but it was a nice thought.

7H. OK, can someone fill me in? What happened today? I mean, I'll admit it, I always knew I was never quite as cool as the kids I hang out with, but for the most part I could overlook that. I mean, they were always pretty nice to me, so I stuck around. When I'm with them I just FEEL cooler. It's weird, but it's like I'm better than all the other kids when I'm hanging out with my friends. I know I'm better than all those Aces and Twos and Threes, even though I might not be quite as popular as most of my friends—but that's why I like them! Maybe they don't think I'm so cool after all. Today they just snubbed me right out of the blue. Usually they want me around, but ever since they started hanging out with this new guy, it's like they don't even acknowledge my existence. It's not like he's that great, though. I don't get it. At lunch, I went up to talk to Ten, and she just said "hi" and kept walking by. I ended up sitting with these Fours. They're OK, I guess, but most of them were pretty strange. They just looked at me and didn't even really talk to me. I just wanted to SCREAM at this one girl, I mean, what is SHE looking at?! Geez, some people have NO manners! One of the girls is in some of my classes, though, and she's nice enough. I never really talked to her before today. Those girls are OK for now, but I'm sure Ten was just in a weird mood. They really do like having me around. I mean, why else would they have kept me around for so long? They are my friends; I'm just blowing this whole thing out of proportion. Tomorrow they'll take me back.

SCENE 3: PASSING IN THE HALLWAYS

(JOKER claps, bell sounds and cards put lunch tables away and exit, leaving JOKER alone onstage.)

JOKER. The sound of the bell marks the time to pass
   And travel through the hallways on the way to class.
   But the rules of this game are not easy to learn:
   You can disrupt the whole system by taking a wrong turn.
   If your value is low, stay close to the walls
   And avoid noisy face cards that parade through the halls.
   Be careful where you stand, and abstain from conversation
   With a card who is higher, who'll resent the confrontation.
   Only friends are safe, but they're hard to find
   When cards pass you by in such aggressive states of mind.

   (JOKER claps hands and action resumes.

   8C enters L and 9H enters R, meeting at some point.)

8C. Hey! Have you taken the physics test yet?

9H. Oh, yeah. It was pretty hard, but if you studied the vocabulary, you should do fine.

   (3C enters R humming a classical music piece and waving his arms like a symphony conductor. He's so caught up in what he is doing, that he nearly bumps into KD, JD and QC who are walking in the opposite direction. KD stops in front of 3C and looks him over and utters a sound of disgust, then the three move around 3C and continue in the direction they were going. They bump directly into 4D, who is carrying his stuffed octopus.)

JD. Nice octopus.

4D. Thanks!!

JD *(making an "L" with forefinger and thumb and placing it on forehead)*. Loser!!!

4D *(walking past them and whispering to the stuffed animal)*. Don't listen to her.

   (6D approaches 6C and 7H.)

6D. Oh, hey there, you guys! *(Bashfully.)* Umm ... I was wondering ... can you come to my party tonight?

6C. Of course! I've been planning on it for two weeks!

6D. Awesome! Hey, Seven, how about you?

7H *(hesitantly)*. You'll have to call me ... I don't know ... Yeah, I guess I can go.

6D. Awesome!

(KS and QH enter L, talking together. KS inadvertently bumps into AH, then pushes him down to the floor.)

KS. Watch where you're going, fag!

AH *(rising slowly)*. You bumped into me.

KS. I wouldn't bother bumping into you.

AH *(approaching KS angrily)*. Excuse me?

KS *(getting up into AH's face)*. You heard me.

(They begin to fight.)

QH *(breaking them up)*. Stop! He's not worth it. *(Looks at AH for a moment, then turns to KS.)* Come on. *(They walk past AH.)*

(Wind chimes sound and action freezes.)

AH. Well, now I know what it feels like to be the scum of the earth. Oh, wait, no, I'm picking up the scum. I hate getting in trouble for no good reason! It wasn't even me who started this! I wouldn't be picking up this trash if it weren't for King throwing crap at me. I wish I knew for one day what it's like. What it's like to be one of them. Carefree, lots of friends and nothing to worry about but the wonderful compliments you'll get on your clothes. Why is it that they can't just accept me for me? Take last night for example. I got a phone call and I couldn't figure out who it was ...

QH. OK, OK ... yeah ... I can do this. Ahem ... ahem ... *(Picks up phone, dials two digits, hangs up, sighs.)* Stop it! Stop it!

You're Queen. What are you doing?! UGH! He probably doesn't even like you anyway. He probably sees right through you. Look at you! You're such a fake. Liar! Whatever *(Determined.)* I'm doing it anyway. King'll never know. How could she? It's not like any of the lower numbers even talk to her anyway. *(Composes herself.)* OK … OK … ahem. *(Picks up phone and dials, still a bit apprehensive.)* Um … hi, Ace?

AH. They said that they really liked me. Can you believe it? Someone noticed me! Today at lunch, I recognized the voice. It was Queen who called me. She was hanging out with her usual crowd—Ten, Jack, Queen and King. But I decided to try and approach her anyway. And you know what happened? She snubbed me! And it was only because King was there. Apparently she didn't like me enough to risk her reputation! If only I was more popular! Then there wouldn't be a problem. People would actually want to hang out with me. They'd worship me just like King. I'd show them! I'd be the most popular guy in school. But … oh, well … what can I do? I'm just an Ace … that's just the way things are.

QH. When you guys marched over to our clique … your little rebellion. I bet you never knew that I didn't mean it when I said, "Go away." Well, maybe the rest of them, but not you. But King was right there … She turned to me, disregarding you and said, "Eww! What is that smell?" And I replied, faking a laugh, "Yeah, heh, eww!" Even then, she gave me a glare before she went back to ridiculing you. *(Pause.)* I couldn't say a word. Do you understand what would have happened to me? No, you couldn't. You're just an Ace. God, who am I kidding? This must be a joke. Who could ever believe a Queen could have a crush on an Ace? Whatever.

KS. You know … sometimes I get really pissed off. Why are there so many losers in the world? Why can't people just act normal? Everyone acts so gay! The people in this school can be wicked retarded. I mean, they do it to themselves—it's not my fault he's a loser—he just is. Hey, I worked hard to be where I am. For God sake, I own this place. I'm in the right crowd, captain of the team and, damn it, I'm the most popular guy in this school! And believe me, it isn't easy. Yeah, everyone wants to be me. But I am more than just a jock and just because I am a jock doesn't mean that I'm stupid. I feel like crap most of the time just like anyone else. But the thing is, I can't show it. I have to make fun of the Twos and Threes and Aces—it's the cool thing to do. I don't know. Maybe I hate them because they have it easy. They never have any pressure on them. That means that no one is around to watch their every move, waiting for them to screw up. What the hell, I'm no better than the Aces I make fun of. I don't understand what I am doing wrong. Someone tell me what the hell I'm doing wrong.

6D. Why am I like this? I invited the face cards to my party. I even printed out directions! They said they would come, but no one did. I thought I was so cool. I guess I'm not. What is it? My hair? My clothes? My music? I wash my hair and I have pretty good clothes, and I thought people liked country music! Maybe I just don't know the right people. I've been trying to get to know them—the Nines and Tens. They won't pay attention to me unless I compliment them. Why should I have to? Why should I have to kiss up to them? They're a bunch of snobs! I don't want to be a snob. If I'm not popular, what am I? Am I a geek? How can a Six be a geek? Maybe I'd rather be a geek than a snob. I noticed that kid in my math class walking down the hall today. He was singing opera! He was enjoying it too. I guess it's because he's a geek and doesn't care what the cool people think. That's it. From now on, I won't care what other people think. If I'm not a geek now, I'll become one tonight.

SCENE 4: END OF THE DAY

(JOKER claps and the bell rings, signifying the end of the school day.)

9H *(running up to 8C with a textbook)*. Wait! You should look
   at the diagram on page 52.

8C. Thanks!

*(Cards exit the stage in small groups and individually, as if
leaving the school building.)*

JOKER. The end of the day is finally here.
   Some leave with joy, and others with fear.
   Released from the confines of these treacherous halls
   Where whispers of bigotry bounce off the walls.
   But the judgment doesn't end with the ring of a bell—
   Or does it? Only time will tell.

*(JOKER claps and cards begin entering the stage as if milling
around the schoolyard getting ready to leave by bus or car.
There are several groupings and individual conversations.*

*4D strolls onstage holding his stuffed octopus; looking
around suspiciously. At the other end of the stage, KD, KS,
QC, JD and 10S are standing together in a group.)*

KD. Look at the dorks on the bus.

QC *(in a mocking tone)*. Bye bye!

4D *(pointing across the stage at the group of face cards)*. The
   enemy approaches from 5 o'clock!

KD *(with distain)*. Right.

KS. Yeah, let's go.

(The two start to leave.)

QC *(to JD and 10S)*. Are you getting a ride with me?

JD. Yeah.

QC. Well, come on!

(QC starts to leave with the other two following.)

KD *(calling over to QC)*. Queen!

QC *(to JD and 10S)*. Wait. *(Walks over to where KD and KS are standing)*. Yeah?

KD. What are you doing after school?

QC. Getting stuff set up for my party.

KD. Well, would you like some help?

QC. Sure!

(8C and 9H approach the group.)

8C *(to QC)*. Hey, do you think maybe you could give us a ride?

QC. I don't think I have enough room in my car. Sorry.

(8C and 9H start to move away from the group as QH approaches.)

QC *(calling out to QH)*. Queen! Do you need a ride? I've got plenty of room.

QH. Sure!

(8C and 9H observe the invitation with obvious frustration.)

8C *(to 9H)*. What's up with that??

(3C, AS and 5S are standing in another group. 6D approaches them.)

6D *(hesitantly to 3C)*. Hey! I was wondering … do you want to … hang at my house?

3C. Why? *(Shaking head in disbelief and walking away.)*

(6C enters and approaches the group.)

6C *(to 5S)*. Hey, what are you doing after school?

5S. Ummm … ummm … not much … why?

6C. Well, if you want to do something, just give me a call—OK?

5S. OK! *(They part.)*

6D *(to 6C)*. Hey, are you still coming?

6C. Yeah. I'm going to come early to help you out.

6D. Awesome!

(Wind chimes sound and action freezes.)

QC. Oh, yeah … of course I'm cool. Don't you know who I am? I hang with the crowd that everyone else wants to hang with. In fact, I'm almost the leader of my group. The only person more popular than me is King—who I think talks about me behind my back. Come to think of it, I have a feeling that my other "friends" don't like me as much as they claim to either. *(Sigh.)* Oh, who am I kidding? I hate this—this fake and superior image, this assumption that I'm better than everyone—for some unknown reason. From watching other people—many of them I had never even really seen before—I decided that their friendships seemed to be more real than the ones I have. They never seem to worry about whether their friends really like them or not. So, I decided a few days ago that I was going to go out and make some new friends—meet some people who they said were "below me." Easy, right? HA! Wrong! Every single group I approached rejected me. I thought everyone wanted to be friends with me! I guess I was wrong. Anyway, eventually, I decided that it was just too frustrating to keep trying to make friends if they just weren't going to accept me. Today I went back to my old group. It was a little weird at first, but by the end of the lunch period everything was back to normal again. I know they'll be off gossiping about all this the first chance they get, but at least they treat me with respect when I'm with them. I guess I belong with those guys, whether I like it or not.

8C. I had to ride the loser cruiser home today. God did I feel like an idiot. I was surrounded by freshmen and littler kids. Hey—at least I'm cooler than them. Eh, I dunno, my ride home must have forgotten to wait for me or something. That happens a lot—no big deal. Like, I'll be waiting outside my house in the morning and eventually I'll look at my watch to find out that I've missed the bus. It turns out that my ride left early and didn't call me. Said he didn't have my number. I coulda sworn I gave it to him, though. Anyways ... I was riding the bus, sitting across from this kid, Two. Now, me and Two used to be close in elementary school, but you know how things are. People start hanging with different people in high school; and two friends, no matter how close, will eventually become separated. But, whatever, he seems to have sunk to the bottom of the social barrel since then. I sort of feel bad for him. But I try to block stuff like that out. Speaking of which, I wonder what I'm doing tonight! There's this party at King's but no one really told me about it. I'll show up anyways, though. Gotta find a ride there. Let's see ... I got Six ... naw ... Ten ... maybe ... yeah, possibly ... Jack, neh, probably got a full car already. Eh, whatever, it will work out. Either that, or I could hang out with Two. *(Laughs.)* Hell, I'm better than that!

5S *(slowly and deliberately)*. They call me "The Dude" ... which doesn't really bother me. In fact ... nothing really bothers me. I'm just *(Pause.)* ... How do I explain it? ... Sometimes people that don't know me think that I must be, you know, contemplating the meaning of life or something ... because I'm so withdrawn. That's not it at all. I just don't care. It's not that I'm lazy, I'm just motivationally challenged. Yeah, I think I like that term ... motivationally challenged. These jocks confuse me. They spend every single afternoon at these long, painful, grueling practices. And then they come home and they don't have time to do anything else. And they always complain about being so busy all the time. That just doesn't make sense to me. I mean ... what do I spend most of my afternoons doing? *(Pauses and searches for the answer.)* I come home from school. *(Pauses and scratches head.)* I usually have some grape soda. Then I sit around for a while ... maybe watch some TV. I watch a lot of TV. Then I drink grape soda again ... and watch a little more TV ... and have some more grape soda.

KD. I am the coolest. Why would I waste my precious time with those so below me? I grace the presence of my friends only because they are cool too … of course, not as cool as me. Why the lower people waste their time trying to be like me is beyond me. They should spend their time doing things they're good at, such as picking up my trash. After all, that's all their good for, right? And that's the perception everyone has of me. There's this role I've been forced into playing. I've been playing it for so long that even I have started to believe that's who I really am. I honestly don't mean to be mean to people. But I have problems too, you know? I have those days where everything makes me cry—school, home-work, boyfriends, the future, the lack of future, the fear of future, fear in general. But it's hard to say what the problem is in the first place. Yeah, I have days like that too.

(Cards form a line across the stage, with the JOKER in front of them facing the audience.)

JOKER. So know you have met our variant cast.
Each struggling to be better than the last.
In order to belong, we distort our ways of seeing,
Place focus on the outer and ignore the inner being.
A school has posed as our example today,
But it's present everywhere: at work, at home, at play.
But what if the values were removed?
Would each person's character be approved?
When you view them all—

9H. Nine

3C. Three

4D. Four

10S. Ten

2S. Two

AS. Ace

6C. Six

JD. Jack

7H. Seven

AH. Ace

QC. Queen

KS. King

6D. Six

QH. Queen

8C. Eight

5S. Five

KD. King

JOKER. Depending on conditions and rules of the game,

  They could be shuffled and rearranged.

  Our request is simply for a change of heart:

  That you, in turn, will do your part

  To consider who you label as worst and best,

  For, in essence, we're all as equal as the next.

  In order to judge what is clear and true,

  Just discard the hand that's been dealt to you.

  (Cards remove outer shirts to reveal plain white T-shirts underneath.)

JOKER *(cont'd)*. Find a house of cards in your own lives:

  The Kings, the Queens, the Aces and Fives,

  And reconsider who you've accessed;

  That, my friends, will be the true test.

  (Music rises as lights fade to black.)

END OF PLAY

MONOLOGUES

For Teachers/Actors: The following monologues can be used for monologue work out of the context of the play or for competition (slight changes have been made to make them stand alone).

JOHN/JESSICA. Right, so anyway … what am I doing? Packing my backpack! Then why … why am I packing a stuffed octopus? I guess this might be why everyone thinks of me as eccentric. You know what? I like being me with my stuffed octopus. Everybody knows you need a stuffed octopus for math class, right? And of course I have Phillip, my lucky penny. Phillip is a girl, by the way. She and I have been together since preschool, and guess what? I haven't even been hit by a bus yet! Seriously! Not a single one! Oh, sure, I have been hit by a few cars, but … the jocks were driving them. Yeah, darn jocks! They are deeply involved in a vast left-wing conspiracy designed to destroy me and the other psychopaths. I know it. But really, who wants friends like them when you're more at peace without them? You know what? Yesterday, I heard Phillip talking. She said she was actually an agent for the FBI and that, when I least expect it, she would turn me in to the feds. I think she is delusional. But she listens when I talk … Yeah, Phillip is truly a lucky penny—at least for now. Watch, tomorrow Rebecca will ridicule me using her third grade vocabulary as we pass each other in the hall. Whatever …

GREG. You should have seen what happened today. Today was awesome … actually it was better than awesome—it rocked! 'Kay, well you know that new girl, Jen or whatever? Yeah, well me, Rachel, Amanda, Karen, Karina and Seth were all just hanging out and stuff, and Jen totally just came over and tried to be all cool … but she just doesn't understand that she's a loser and will never be able to hang out with us. So when she came over, I saw this as an opportunity to try and heighten

32

my status with Seth, so I made my move and told Jen that her face looked like a war zone of acne, and Jen totally walked away from us … it was a really good move on my part, cuz the group totally thought I was cool for it, which pretty much guaranteed myself a spot at the table later in the week at lunch. Adam confronted me the other day and wanted to know why I haven't been hanging out with the theatre crowd lately, and I just told Adam that I didn't like them anymore and did not feel appreciated by them … but the truth is, I never felt under-appreciated or disliked by drama geeks … or really by anyone below me, I always felt awesome. They're all really cool and really nice, but they don't understand … no one understands … there's always been something missing. Whenever I saw any of the popular kids walking in the hall, they always looked different. They always looked special—like they were set apart from everyone else. They always looked so glamorous and, well, famous to an extent … famous in our school, I mean. And all that I wanted was a piece of what they had. And I found the way … I have finally found the key to walking with them in the halls, sitting with them at lunch, going to the mall on weekends … why should I give that up now? I do miss them, though …Adam and Hannah … and even Amy a little … but I can't … that phase, that section of my life is done. What would Seth and the others think? *(Sigh.)* Later I'm going over to Jack's house—we're going to watch TRL together. God, I hate that show, but imagine … me … at Jack's house! I'll pretend to like it, so that the group doesn't kick me out … then I won't have anybody to sit with at lunch … well, except for Brian, but hell—I don't think even the math team would sit with Brian!

LISA *(looking at Hannah).* I wonder what it would be like … to be her. I wonder how I would wake up in the morning. Would my hair be perfect and my make-up pre-applied? Would I look in the mirror and say, "Wow! I look hot today"?

Would I know that I would be the dream and the envy of every single person around me? Would I know that I would be worshipped and praised by people like me? That I'm wonderful? That I am the most powerful person in the school? All my friends think I am so strong. They think I don't care what people say about me. I guess I would think the same if a friend of mine acted the way I do, always denouncing their superiority. "Who cares if they call me gorilla, right? Who cares if they call me the beast? They're not that wonderful anyway."—I wonder if anyone knows how I really feel; if they know that I would do anything to be like that, like her. I would kill.

AMY. I am outta here … this school sucks! I don't care what you think I should wear or who I should be friends with or what I like to do with my free time or what party I am NOT invited to this weekend or why I have no boyfriend or why my parents love my sister more than me or any of it … I'm just so tired. So tired of all this … I feel like all I do is try to impress people and try to be what everyone wants me to be and I am so mixed up that I don't even know who that is or was, or whatever. And I have too much homework and I hate my math teacher and I have no dress to wear to the Spring Fling and my friends all have a different lunch periods so I am stuck between the school council members and the pot-heads and drop outs without a place to sit. Can't hang with the cheerleaders—not good enough for them and I am NOT gonna be caught with the losers. This year is just like last year—same old crap, different day. I don't think I can take much more of this. My life pretty much sucks. Pretty much.

PETER. I had to ride the loser cruiser home today. God, did I feel like an idiot. I was surrounded by freshmen and littler kids. Hey, at least I'm cooler than them. Eh, I dunno, my ride home must have forgotten to wait for me or something. That happens a lot—no big deal. Like, I'll be waiting outside my house in the morning and eventually I'll look at my watch to find out that I've missed the bus. It turns out that my ride left early and didn't call me. Said he didn't have my number. I coulda sworn I gave it to him, though. Anyways ... I was riding the bus, sitting across from this kid, Michael. Now, me and Michael used to be close in elementary school, but you know how things are. People start hanging with different people in high school; and two friends, no matter how close, will eventually become separated. But, whatever, he seems to have sunk to the bottom of the social barrel since then. I sort of feel bad for him. But I try to block stuff like that out. Speaking of which, I wonder what I'm doing tonight! There's this party at Seth's but no one really told me about it. I'll show up anyways, though. Gotta find a ride there. Let's see ... I got Tony ... naw ... Greg ... maybe ... yeah, possibly ... Jack, neh, probably got a full car already. Eh, whatever, it will work out. Either that, or I could hang out with Michael. *(Laughs.)* Hell, I'm better than that!

NOTES

NOTES

NOTES

NOTES

NOTES